Irish Culture and Customs Book of Jokes

Edited by Russell Haggerty

For my wife Bridget.
June 14th, 1946—June 4th, 2017
May she rest in Peace.
She was and still is the love of my life

Introduction

Irish Culture and Customs.com was started by Bridget and Russell Haggerty in June of 2002.

Over the years it has grown to about 700 pages divided into seven departments.

Bridget Haggerty was the guiding light and driving force through all those years.

Bridget passed away in June of 2017. Russell continues to maintain everything as best he can.

This is one of a series of books based on the content of Irish Culture and Customs.

When they are finally complete most of the content will be preserved in book form.

I hope you enjoy all of them.

Blessings to you all
Russ Haggerty

Have you heard about the Irish boomerang?It doesn't come back, it just sings sad songs about how much it wants to.

ॐ

Mike wakes up at home with a huge hangover. He forces himself to open his eyes, and the first thing he sees are a couple of aspirins and a glass of water on the bedside table. He sits up in bed and sees his clothing in front of him, all clean and ironed. He looks around the room and sees that it is in perfect order, spotless. He takes the aspirins and sees a note on the table which says 'Breakfast is on the stove, dear. I left early to go shopping. Love you!' He goes to the kitchen and sure enough, there's a hot breakfast waiting for him, and also the morning newspaper. His son is sitting at the table, eating. Really curious by now, Mike asks, "Son, what happened last night?" His son says, "Well, Mam said you came home after 3 a.m, you stumbled in the door, threw up in the hallway, and passed out half-way up the stairs." Confused, Mike asks, "So, why is everything in order and so clean, and breakfast is on the table waiting for me?" His son replies, "Oh, that! Mam dragged you to the bedroom, and when she tried to take your trousers off, you yelled 'Leave me alone woman, I'm a married man'".

A woman awakes during the night to find that her husband was not in their bed. She puts on her robe and goes downstairs to look for him. She finds him sitting at the kitchen table with a cup of coffee in front of him. He appears deep in thought, just staring at the wall. She watches as he wipes a tear from his eye and takes a sip of coffee. "What's the matter, dear?" she whispers as she steps into the room, "Why are you down here at this time of night?" "Do you remember when I met you and you were only 16?" he asks solemnly. The wife is touched to tears thinking that her husband is so caring and sensitive. "Yes, I do" she replies. The husband pauses. The words are not coming easily. "Do you remember when your father caught us in the back seat of my car, making love?" "Yes, I remember" says the wife, lowering herself into a chair beside him. The husband continues... "Do you remember when he shoved a shotgun in my face and said, "Either you marry my daughter, or I will send you to jail for 20 years?'" "I remember that too" she replies softly. He wipes another tear from his cheek and says... "I would have gotten out today."

An unfortunate slip recently occurred at a wedding breakfast in Killarney, Co. Kerry. The happy pair had been toasted in the usual way. Then a general conversation took place, which related to the nuisance of children being present at social gatherings - especially weddings. A happy idea struck the bridegroom. "Why not have it mentioned on the invitation cards?" said he. "For instance, we could have had on ours No Children Expected." A long silence followed, until somebody remarked that the weather was remarkable for this time of year.

A garda pulls over a speeding car. He says, "I clocked you at 80 miles per hour, sir." The driver says, "Are you sure? I had it on cruise control at 60, perhaps your radar gun needs calibrating." Not looking up from her knitting the wife says: "Now don't be silly dear, you know that this car doesn't have cruise control." As the garda writes out the ticket, the driver looks over at his wife and growls, "Can't you please keep your mouth shut for once?" The wife smiles demurely and says, "You should be thankful your radar detector went off when it did." As the garda makes out the second ticket for the illegal use of a radar detector unit*, the man glowers at his wife and says through clenched teeth, "Woman didn't I tell you to keep your mouth shut!" The garda frowns and says "And I notice that you're not wearing your seat belt, sir. That's an on the spot 60 euro fine." The driver says, "Well, you see sir, I had it on, but took it off when you pulled me over so that I could get my license out of my back pocket." The wife says, "Now, dear, you know very well that you didn't have your seat belt on. You never wear your seat belt when you're driving." And as the garda is writing out the third ticket the driver turns to his wife and barks, "WHY DON'T YOU PLEASE SHUT UP??" The garda looks over at the woman and asks, "Does your husband always talk to you this way, Ma'am?" Smiling sweetly, she replies. "Only when he's been drinking, sir".

*While it is legal to own a radar detector in the Republic of Ireland, it is actually illegal to use it.

Miss O'Leary, the church organist, was in her eighties and had never been married. She was much admired for her sweetness and kindness to all. The parish priest came to call on her one afternoon early in the spring, and she welcomed him into her little cottage. She invited him to have a seat while she made the tea. As he sat facing her old pump organ, the priest noticed a cut glass bowl sitting on top of it, filled with water. In the water floated, of all things, an item the menfolk use to help prevent conception. Imagine his shock and surprise. Imagine his curiosity! Surely Miss O'Leary had lost her senses! When she returned with the tea and scones, they began to chat. The priest tried to stifle his curiosity about the bowl of water and its unusual contents, but soon it got the better of him; he could resist no longer. Miss O'Leary," he said, "I wonder if you would tell me about this?" (pointing to the bowl). "Oh, yes, Father," she replied, "Isn't it wonderful? I was walking in the village last October and I found this little package on the ground. The directions said to put it on the organ, keep it wet, and it would prevent disease. And you know... I haven't had a cold all winter."

The rich American couldn't understand why the Irish angler was lying lazily beside his boat on the beach, smoking a pipe. "Why aren't you out fishing?" asked the American. "Because I have caught enough fish for the day," said the fisherman. "Why don't you catch some more?" "What would I do with them?" "You could sell them and make more money," was the American's reply. "With that you could have a motor fixed to your boat and go into deeper waters and catch more fish. Then you would make enough to buy nets. These would bring you more fish and more money. Soon you would have enough money to own two boats . . . maybe even a fleet of boats. Then you would be a rich man like me." "What would I do then?" asked the fisherman. "Then you could really enjoy life." said the American. "And what do you suppose I might be doing right now?" said the Irishman, smiling and puffing away on his pipe.

Sean was a mild-mannered man who was tired of being hen-pecked by his wife; so he went to a psychiatrist. The psychiatrist said he needed to build his self-esteem and gave him a book on assertiveness. Sean read the book on the bus home. By the time he reached his house, he had finished it. He stormed into the house and walked up to his wife. Pointing a finger in her face, he said, "Bridie, from now on, I want you to know that I am the man of the house, and my word is law! I want you to make my favourite boiled beef and cabbage for the meal tonight and when I'm finished with that, I expect my favourite whiskey cake for afters. Then, you're going to draw me my bath so I can relax. And when I'm finished with that, do you know who's going to dress me and comb my hair?" "The undertaker." says she.

After just a few years of marriage filled with constant bickering, the Kerry couple decided the only way to save their marriage was to try counseling. When they arrived at the counselor's office, the counselor jumped right in and opened the floor for discussion. "What seems to be the problem?" Immediately, the husband held his long face down without anything to say. In contrast, the wife began talking 90 miles an hour, describing all the wrongs within their marriage. After 15 minutes of listening to the wife, the counselor went over to her, picked her up by her shoulders, kissed her passionately and sat her back down. Afterwards, the wife sat speechless. The marriage counselor looked over at the husband, who stared in disbelief.

The counselor said to the husband, "Your wife NEEDS that at least twice a week!" The husband scratched his head and replied, "I can have her here on Tuesdays and Thursdays."

Sean calls home to his wife and says, "Aiofe, I have been asked to go fishing on Lough Ree with my boss and several of his friends. We'll be gone for a week. This is a good opportunity for me to get that promotion I've been wanting so would you please pack me enough clothes for a week and set out my rod and tackle box. We're leaving from the office and I'll stop by the house to pick them up. Oh, and, please pack my new blue silk pajamas."Aiofe thinks this all sounds a little fishy but being a good wife she does exactly what her husband asked. The following weekend he comes home a little tired but otherwise looking good. The wife welcomes him home and asks if he caught many fish? He says, "Yes! Lot's of trout, some salmon, and a few pike. But why didn't you pack my new blue silk pajamas like I asked you to do?" "I did, Sean; they're in your tackle box."

A woman goes to the post office to stock up on stamps. She says to the clerk, "May I have 50 stamps please?" The clerk says, "What denomination?" The woman says, "God bless us, has it come to that? I'll have 18 Protestants, and 32 Catholics."

An elderly Kerry couple is sitting together watching television. During one of 'those' commercials, the husband asked his wife, "Whatever happened to our sexual relations?" After a long thoughtful silence (and during the next commercial), the wife replied, "You know, I don't know. I don't even think we got a Christmas card from them this year."

Maureen's husband, Patrick, was a typical Irish male chauvinist. Even though they both worked full-time, he never helped around the house. Housework was woman's work! But one evening, Maureen arrived home to find the children bathed, one load of clothes in the washer and another in the dryer, dinner on the stove, and the table set. She was astonished; something's up, she thought.It turns out that Patrick had read an article that said wives who worked full-time and also had to do all the housework were too tired to make love.The night went well and the next day she told her office friends all about it. “We had a great dinner. Patrick even cleaned up. He helped the kids do their homework, folded all the laundry and put everything away. I really enjoyed the evening.” “But what about afterward?” asked her friends. “Oh, that was perfect, too. Patrick was too tired!”

A gorgeous young redhead goes into the doctor’s office and says that her body hurts wherever she touches it. “Impossible!” says the doctor. “Show me.” The redhead takes her finger, pushes on her left breast and screams, then she pushes her elbow and screams in even more agony. She pushes her knee and screams; likewise she pushes her ankle and screams. Everywhere she touches makes her scream. The doctor says, “You’re not really a redhead, are you? “Well, no” she says, “I’m actually a blonde.” “I thought so,” the doctor says. “Your finger is broken.”

Mrs. O'Leary went to the doctor's office where she was seen by one of the new physicians. After about 4 minutes in the examination room, she burst out the door and ran screaming down the hall. An older doctor stopped her and asked what the problem was, and she told him her story. After listening, he had her sit down and relax in another room.The older doctor marched down the hallway to the back where the first doctor was and demanded, "What's the matter with you? Mrs. O'Leary is 72 years old, she has seven grown children and ten grandchildren, and you told her she was pregnant?" The new doctor continued to write on his clipboard and without looking up said, "Does she still have the hiccups?"

Costigan from Cork was marooned on a desert island where he was looked after by a beautiful native girl. On the first night she gave him exotic drinks. On the second night she gave him the most delicious food. On the third night she said to him coyly "Would you like to play a little game with me?" "Don't tell me," he says, "you have hurling here as well?"

One morning at the bargaining table, the company's chief negotiator held aloft the morning edition of the Cork Examiner. "This man," he announced, "Called in sick yesterday!" There on the sports page was a photo of the supposedly ill employee, who had just won a local golf tournament with an excellent score. The silence in the room was broken by a union negotiator. "Jaysus," he said. "Think of the score he could have had if he hadn't been sick!"

A Kerry man went for a job at the local stables and the farmer said "Can you shoe horses?" The Kerry man thinks for a minute and then says "No, but I once told a donkey to get lost."

A teacher was testing the children in her Sunday school class to see if they understood the concept of getting into heaven. She asked them, "If I sold my house and my car, had a big rummage sale and gave all my money to the church, would that get me into Heaven?"

"NO!" the children answered. "If I cleaned the church every day, cut the grass, and kept everything tidy, would that get me into Heaven?" Again, the answer was, "NO!" By now the teacher was starting to smile - this was fun! "Well, then, if I was kind to animals and gave sweets to all the children, and loved my husband, would that get me into Heaven?" Again, they all answered, "NO!" Bursting with pride for them, the teacher continued: "So, how can I get into Heaven?" Five-year-old Sean shouted out, "YOU HAVE TO BE DEAD."

John Smith was the only Protestant to move into a large Catholic neighborhood. On the first Friday of Lent, John was outside grilling a big juicy steak on his grill. Meanwhile, all of his neighbors were fixing fish. This went on each Friday of Lent. On the last Friday of Lent, the neighborhood men got together and decided that something had to be done about John - he was tempting them to eat meat each Friday of Lent, and they couldn't take it anymore. They decided to try and convert John to be a Catholic. They went over and talked to him and were so happy that he decided to join all of his neighbors and become a Catholic. They took him to Church, and the Priest sprinkled some water over him, and said, "You were born a Baptist, you were raised a Baptist, and now you are a Catholic." The men were so relieved, now their biggest Lenten temptation was resolved. The next year's Lenten season rolled around. The first Friday of Lent came, and just at supper time, when the neighborhood was sitting down to their fish dinner, came the wafting smell of steak cooking on a grill. The neighborhood men could not believe their noses! WHAT WAS GOING ON? They called each other up and decided to meet over at John's place to see if he had forgotten it was the first Friday of Lent. The group arrived just in time to see John standing over his grill with a small pitcher of water. He was sprinkling some water over his steak on the grill, saying, "You were born a cow, you were raised a cow, and now you are a fish."

A Kerryman was playing Trivial Pursuit. It was his turn. He rolled the dice and landed on "Science & Nature." His question was, "If you are in a vacuum and someone calls your name, can you hear it?" He thought for a time and then asked, "Is it on or off?"

When my older brother was very young, he always walked up to the church altar with my mother when she took communion. On one occasion, he tugged at her arm and asked, “What does the priest say when he gives you the bread?” Mom whispered something in his ear. Imagine his shock many years later when he learned that the priest doesn’t say, “Be quiet until you get to your seat.”

Sean is walking through the park and notices an old lady sitting on a bench sobbing her eyes out. He stops and asks her what is wrong. She says, “I have a 22-year old husband at home. He kisses and cuddles me every morning and then gets up and makes me eggs, bacon, black pudding, toast and tea.” Well then,” Sean says, “Why are you crying?” She says, “He makes me homemade soup for lunch and then kisses and cuddles me for half the afternoon.” Perplexed, Sean says, “So, why are you crying?” She says, “For supper, he always makes me my favourite meal and then kisses and cuddles me until 2:00 a.m.

Astonished by now, Sean says, “Why in the world would you be crying, then?” Says she, “I can’t remember where I live!”

Sean goes into the pub and asks for three Guinness. He sits there and sips from the first one, then the second, and the third. He does this until finally all three pints are finished. He pays the bill and leaves. A couple of nights later he comes back and repeats the ritual. This goes on for a while and finally the bartender’s curiosity gets the better of him and he asks why the three Guinness and why drink them all together the way he does. “Well, “ says Sean, “My brother Michael is in the USA and my other brother Liam is in Australia. We can’t meet in the pub and share a Guinness, so we have an agreement that whenever we go have a drink, we order three pints and pretend we’re together.” The bartender thinks to himself, “What a wonderful idea.” A few months go by and one night Sean comes in and he orders two Guinness. The bartender is afraid to ask, but Sean seems fine, so finally the bartender says, “I see you’ve only ordered two Guinness tonight. Did something happen to one of your brothers?” “No, no,” says Sean, “They’re both fit as a fiddle and healthy as horses!” “So why only the two Guinness?" asks the bartender. "Ah, well now," says Sean, "I've given up Guinness for Lent."

A surgeon and an architect, both English, were joined by an Irish politician and all fell to arguing as to whose profession was the oldest. Said the surgeon, "Eve was made from Adam's rib, and that surely was a surgical operation." "Maybe," said the architect, "but prior to that, order was created out of chaos, and that was an architectural job." "Sure now," interrupted the politician, "but wasn't somebody after creating the chaos first?"

A pompous priest was seated next to an Irishman on a flight home.After the plane was airborne, drink orders were taken. The Irishman asked for an Irish whiskey. The attendant placed the drink on his tray and then asked the priest if he would like a drink. He replied in disgust," I'd rather be savagely ravaged by brazen hussies than let alcohol touch my lips."The Irishman then handed his drink back to the attendant and said "Me too. I didn't know we had a choice!"

After Mass one Sunday, Miss O'Leary went up to the priest and said, "I have to tell you Father, your sermons are a wonder to behold. Sure we didn't know what sin was till you came to the parish!"

The first priest says, "You know, since the warm weather started, I've been having trouble with mice in my church. I've tried everything - noise, cats, spray, nothing seems to scare them away." The second priest says, "My church, too. There are hundreds of them living in the cellar. I've set traps and even called in an expert exterminator. Nothing has worked so far." The third priest says, "I had the same problem. So I baptized them all and made them members of my parish. Haven't seen one of them since."

While impatiently waiting for a table in a restaurant, Miss O'Leary says to Mrs. Clancy, "If they weren't so crowded in here all the time, they'd do a lot more business."

A man walked into the lingerie department of Dunnes in Dublin and said to the woman behind the counter, “I’d like to buy a Baptist bra for my wife, size 36B.” What type of bra? asked the clerk. “Baptist” said the man. She said get a Baptist bra, and that you’d know what she meant.” “Ah yes, now I remember” said the saleslady. “We don’t sell many of those. Mostly our customers want the Catholic type, the Salvation Army type. or the Presbyterian type.” Confused the man asked, “What’s the difference between them?” The lady responded, “It is all really quite simple; the Catholic type supports the masses, the Salvation Army type lifts up the fallen, and the Presbyterian type keeps them staunch and upright. Then there’s the Baptist type.” “What does that do?” asked the man. She replied, “It makes mountains out of molehills.”

The spring bank holiday was over and the teacher asked the class how they had spent the time. Kevin eagerly put up his hand. “We visited our cousins in Carrigaline!” “Well, Kevin,” says the teacher, “that sounds like a brilliant vocabulary word - can you tell the class how to spell Carrigaline?” Kevin furrowed his brow, chewed on his lip, and then said with a big grin, “Em, well now, come to think of it, we went to Cork!”

A man and a woman, who have never met before, find themselves assigned to the same sleeping room on a transcontinental train. Though initially embarrassed and uneasy over sharing a room, the two are tired and fall asleep quickly - he in the upper bunk and she in the lower. At 2:00AM, he leans over and gently wakes the woman, saying, “Ma’am, I’m sorry to bother you, but would you be willing to reach into the cupboard to get me a second blanket? I’m awfully cold.” “I have a better idea,” she replies. “Just for tonight, let’s pretend that we’re married.” “That’s a great idea!” he exclaims. “Good,” she replies. “Get up and get your own blanket.”

Two men walked into a pub late one afternoon and noticed that, among the few customers, was one individual sitting quietly at the end of the bar. The two ordered some beers. The bartender brought them and said, "that will be 50p please." They put it on the slate and a short time later ordered two more beers; again they were charged 25p each. The two could not believe the price and after having a third beer for the same amount, they decided to ask the bartender what the catch was. The bartender replied, "there is no catch, gentlemen. I have just started brewing this beer on the premises and I'm selling it below cost to introduce it to my customers. I'm happy to see you're enjoying it." Indeed, they noticed that almost everyone was enjoying the beer and the remarkable price except for the one man at the end of the bar. He had not ordered anything since the two came in. Becoming very curious about this individual, the two asked the bartender, "Doesn't he ever order anything?" "Oh yes," said the bartender. "That's Patrick Curran, our local accountant. He's waiting for happy hour."

An Irishman died and went to heaven. As he

stood in front of St. Peter at the Pearly Gates, he saw a huge wall of clocks behind him. He asked, "What are all those clocks?" St. Peter answered, "Those are Lie-Clocks. Everyone in the universe has a Lie-Clock. Every time you lie, the hands on your clock will move." "Oh," said the man, "whose clock is that?" "That's St. Patrick's. The hands have never moved, indicating that he never told a lie." "Incredible," said the man. "And whose clock is that one?" St. Peter responded, "That's Daniel O'Connell's clock. The hands have moved twice, telling us that he told only two lies in his entire life." "Where's Bertie Ahern's clock?" asked the man. "Bertie's clock is in God's office. He's using it as a ceiling fan."

Three men were sitting together bragging about how they had set their new wives straight on their domestic duties. The first man had married a woman from Italy and boasted that he had told his wife she was to do all the dishes and house cleaning that needed to be done. He said that it took a couple days but on the third day he came home to a clean house and the dishes were all washed and put away. The second man had married a woman from France. He bragged that he had given his wife orders that she was to do all the cleaning, all the dishes, and the cooking. He told them that the first day he didn't see any results, but the next day it was better. By the third day, his house was clean, the dishes were done, and he had a delicious dinner on the. table. The third man had married an Irish girl. He boasted that he told her his house was to be cleaned, the dishes washed, the cooking done and the laundry washed. And this was all entirely her responsibility. He said the first day he didn't see anything and the second day he didn't see anything, but by the third day some of the swelling had gone down so he could see a little out of his left eye!

A curious fellow died one day and found himself waiting in the long line of judgment. As he stood there he noticed that some souls were allowed to march right through the pearly gates into Heaven. Others though, were led over to Satan who threw them into the burning pit. But every so often, instead of hurling a poor soul into the fire, Satan would toss a soul off to one side into a small pile. After watching Satan do this several times, the fellow's curiosity got the best of him. So he strolled over and asked Satan what he was doing. "Excuse me, Prince of Darkness," he said. "I'm waiting in line for judgment, but I couldn't help wondering, why are you tossing those people aside instead of flinging them into the Fires of Hell with the others?" "Ah, those ...Satan said with a groan. "They're all from Ireland. They're still too cold and damp to burn."

Mrs. O'Reilly returned home from a vacation to France where she had taken a cooking class. She tells her husband Paddy she is going to prepare him a special meal and he is to go down to Sean's Market and buy two dozen escargot, which she explains to Paddy are snails. Mrs. O'Reilly admonishes Paddy to come right home, no stops at the pub, because she wants to have escargot for dinner. Paddy buys the snails and is on his way home but alas, his route takes him right by his favorite pub. Just one he tells himself. Well, perhaps another he says after having the first pint. The company is good, the tales are tall, and Paddy finds himself having three or four. As Paddy heads home he realizes it has become dark and knows his lovely wife will be waiting and sharpening her tongue for him. As Paddy opens the gate to home the porch light comes on and he hears the door begin to open. Paddy empties the bag of escargot on the ground and says in a loud voice "Come on now lads! You're almost there."

The man from the window company called Miss O'Leary on the telephone. "Miss O'Leary, he says, you haven't made a single payment on your new windows. Is there something the matter?" Bristling with annoyance, Miss O'Leary replies. "I may be up in years, but I still have my wits about me. Wasn't your man after telling me those windows would pay for themselves in a year?"

We can’t win at home, we can’t win away. As general manager, I just can’t figure out where else to play. Jock Brown - Celtic General Manager.

Twins Jack and Sarah were always squabbling. Tired of listening to them yelling at each other and knowing full well neither one would admit they were in the wrong, their mother says, “I have an idea: Sarah, why don’t you tell Jack you were wrong, and Jack, you tell Sarah she was right. So, Sarah says to Jack “I was wrong.” Jack grins and says to Sarah: “You are right.”

Two lovely old biddies had been friends for many decades. Over the years they had shared all kinds of activities and adventures. Lately, their activities had been limited to meeting a few times a week for a cup of tea and a natter. One day they were sipping their tea when one looked at the other and said, "Now don't go getting upset with me...I know we've been pals for a long time.....but I just can't think of your name! I've thought and thought, but I can't remember it. Please tell me what your name is. Her friend glared at her. For at least three minutes she just stared and glared. At last, she said, "How soon do you need to know?

A young lad had just gotten his provisional license. (learner's permit) He asked his father, who was a minister, if they could discuss his use of the car. His father said to him, "If you bring your marks up, study your bible, and get your hair cut, we'll talk about it." A month later the boy came back and again asked his father if they could now discuss his use of the car. His father said, "Well, son, I see that your marks have improved, you've studied your bible diligently, but you didn't get a hair cut!" The young man waited a moment and then replied, “You know dad, I’ve been thinking about that. Didn’t Samson have long hair, Moses have long hair, Noah have long hair, and even Jesus himself have long hair?” His father replied, “They did so, and they walked everywhere they went!”

Morris walks out into the street and hails a taxi just going by. He gets into the taxi, and the cabbie says, “Perfect timing. You’re just like Liam.” “Who?” “Liam O’Connor. There’s a lad who did everything right. Like my coming along when you needed a cab. It would have happened like that to Liam.” “Every path has its puddle” says Morris.” “It wasn’t like that with Liam,” says the cabbie. “He was a brilliant athlete. He could have played football for Kerry. He could golf with the pros. He sang like Ronan Tynan and he danced like Michael Flatley. What’s more, he had a memory like Methusalah. He could remember everyone’s birthday. He knew all about wine, which fork to eat with. He could fix anything. Not like me. I change a fuse, and the whole town goes out.” “No wonder you remember him.” says Morris. “Well, I never actually met the man.” “Then how do you know so much about him?” asks Morris. “I married his widow."

Mrs. Pete Monaghan came into the newsroom to pay for her husband's obituary. She was told by the kindly newsman that it was dollar a word and he remembered Pete and wasn't it too bad about him passing away. She thanked him for his kind words and bemoaned the fact that she only had two dollars. But she wrote out the obituary, "Pete died." The newsman said he thought old Pete deserved more and he'd give her three more words at no charge. Mrs. Pete Monaghan thanked him and rewrote the obituary: 'Pete died. Boat for sale'.

Miss O'Leary was certain her horse would win the big race at the Curragh because the bookie told her it would start at twenty to one and the race didn't begin until a quarter past.

Pat and Mike are drinking in the done-up version of their local pub, The Continental Bistro and Bar in the Ballybegorrah Arms Hotel, Killarney. They take in the no-sawdust on the new Italian tile floor; the hi-back red leather bar stools; the bowls of free black olives, cashew nuts and tasty "tapas" on the shiny, black, two inch thick, granite counter. "Ye know", Pat," says Mike, "it's all brilliant, but I miss the auld spittoon." Pat takes his pipe from his mouth, sips his pint, then says, "You always did, me auld friend. You always did."

While working on a lesson in world religions, a kindergarten teacher asked her students to bring something related to their family's faith to class. At the appropriate time, she asked the students to come forward and share with the rest of the students. The first child said, "I am Muslim, and this is my prayer rug."The second child said, "I am Jewish, and this is my Star of David."The third child said, "I am Catholic, and this is my rosary."The final child said, "I am Protestant, and this is my casserole dish."

An Irish lady goes to the bar on a cruise ship and orders a Jameson with two drops of water. As the bartender gives her the drink she says, “I’m on this cruise to celebrate my 80th birthday and it’s today.” The bartender says, “Well, since it’s your birthday, I’ll buy you a drink. In fact, this one is on me.” “Well, thank you kindly, sir” says she. As the woman finishes her drink, the woman to her right says, “I would like to buy you a drink, too.” The old woman says, “Thank you. Bartender, I’ll have a Jameson with two drops of water.” “Coming up,” says the bartender. As she finishes that drink, the man to her left says, “I would like to buy you one, too.” The old woman says, “Thank you. Bartender, I’ll have another Jameson with two drops of water.” “Coming right up,” the bartender says. As he gives her the drink, he says, “Ma’am, I’m dying of curiosity. Why the Jameson with only two drops of water?” The old woman replies, “Ah, lad, when you’re my age, you’ve learned how to hold the hard stuff. Holding your water, however, is another matter entirely.”

Q: How many Irishmen does it take to change a light bulb?A: Three. One to hold the bulb, one to screw it in, and one to say how grand the old one was.

Father Murphy went out one Saturday to visit his parishioners. At one house it was obvious that someone was home, but nobody came to the door even though the priest had knocked several times. Finally, he took out his card and wrote 'Revelations 3:20' on the back of it, and stuck it in the door: 'Behold, I stand at the door and knock. If anyone hears my voice and opens the door, I will come in to him and dine with him and him with me.' The next day, the card turned up in the collection plate. Below Father Murphy's message was the notation 'Genesis 3:10': 'I heard your voice in the garden and I was afraid because I was naked; and I hid myself.'

Sir Boyle Roche, MP for Co. Kerry was notorious for his oratorical blunders. Witness this lovely example: During the French Revolution, he warned that the revolutionaries might invade Ireland. "Sir," he declaimed, "they would break in, cut us to mince meat and throw our bleeding heads on that table to stare us in the face. Who would not answer such a call to arms, not to mention legs and feet?"

A man was brought to Mercy Hospital, and taken quickly in for coronary surgery. The operation went well and, as the groggy man regained consciousness, he was reassured by a Sister of Mercy, who was waiting by his bed. "Mr. O'Toole, you're going to be just fine," said the nun, gently patting his hand. "We do need to know, however, how you intend to pay for your stay here. Are you covered by insurance?" "No, sorry, I don't have any insurance," the man whispered hoarsely. "Can you pay in cash?" asked the nun. "I'm afraid I cannot, Sister." "Well, do you have any close relatives?" the nun persisted. "Just my sister in America" he volunteered. "But she's a humble spinster nun." "Oh, I must correct you, Mr. O'Toole. Nuns are not 'spinsters;' they are married to God." "Wonderful," said O'Toole. "In that case, please send the bill to my brother-in-law."

Attending a wedding for the first time, a little girl whispered to her mother, “Why is the lady all dressed in white?” “Because white is the color of happiness, and today is the happiest day of her life. The child thought about this for a moment, then said, “So why is the man wearing black?”

An elderly woman died last month. Having never married, she requested no male pallbearers. In her handwritten instructions for her memorial service, she wrote, “They wouldn’t take me out while I was alive, I don’t want them to take me out when I’m dead.”

“Which is the first and most important sacrament?” asked the Catechism teacher. “Marriage”, avowed Moira. “No, baptism is the first and most important sacrament,” corrected the teacher. “Not in our family,” retorted Moira, in a haughty voice. “We’re decent people!”

Charlie was a regular visitor at the Galway Races. One afternoon he noticed an unusual sight. Right before the first race, a Catholic priest visited one of the horses in the stable area and gave it a blessing. Charlie watched the race very carefully, and sure enough the blessed horse came in first! Charlie followed the priest before the next race, and again he went to the stables and performed a similar procedure. Thinking there might be something to it, Charlie put a couple of euros on the blessed horse. Sure enough it came in by two lengths and Charlie won close to fifty euros! The priest continued the same procedure through the next few races and Charlie won each time. He was now ahead a thousand, so between races Charlie left the track, went to the bank and withdrew his life's savings. The biggest race of the day was the last one. Charlie followed the priest and watched which horse he blessed. He then went to the betting window and put every euro he owned on that horse to win. The race began. Down the stretch they came, and as they crossed the finish line, Charlie's pick was last! Devastated, he found the priest and told him that he had been watching him bless the horses all day, and they all became winners except the last horse on which he had bet his life savings. Charlie then asked, "What happened to the last horse which you blessed? Why didn't it win like the others?" "Ye must be a Protestant," sighed the priest. "The trouble is you can't tell the difference between a blessing and the last rites."

A wealthy couple from Texas were touring Ireland and found themselves in a tiny rural village at lunchtime. The only place serving food was a somewhat rustic looking cafe which in their opinion, had seen better days. Having no other choice, they carefully stepped over the pooch snoozing on the threshold and went inside. As they sat down, the husband frowned as he brushed some crumbs from his chair and his wife did likewise as she wiped the table with her napkin.The waitress came over and asked if they would like to see a menu. "No thanks," said the husband. "I'll just have a cup of tea with cream and sugar." "I'll have the same", his wife said. "And please make sure the cup is clean." Unphased by the rudeness of the remark, the waitress smiled and marched off into the kitchen. A few minutes later, she was back. "Two cups of tea," she announced in her lovely lilting Irish brogue...And which one of you was it who wanted the clean cup?"

It's a wee bit lengthy, but worth the read.There were two nuns. One of them was known as Sister Mathematical (SM), and the other one was known as Sister Logical (SL). It is getting dark and they are still far away from the convent. SM: Have you noticed that a man has been following us for the past thirty-eight and a half minutes? I wonder what he wants. SL: "It's logical. He wants to have his way with us." SM: "Oh, no! At this rate he will reach us in 15 minutes at the most! What can we do?" SL: "The only logical thing to do is to walk faster." SM: "It's not working." SL: "Of course it's not working. The man did the only logical thing. He started to walk faster, too." SM: "So, what shall we do? At this rate he will reach us in one minute." SL: "The only logical thing we can do is split up. You go that way and I'll go this way. He cannot follow us both." So the man decided to follow Sister Logical. Sister Mathematical arrives at the convent and is worried about what has happened to Sister Logical. Then Sister Logical arrives.SM: "Sister Logical! Thank God you are here! Tell me what happened!" SL: "The only logical thing happened. The man couldn't follow us both, so he followed me." SM: "Yes, yes! But what happened then?" SL: "The only logical thing happened. I started to run as fast as I could and he started to run as fast as he could." SM: "And?" SL: "The only logical thing happened. He reached me." SM: "Oh, dear! What did you do?" SL: "The only logical thing to do. I lifted my habit up." SM: "Oh, Sister! What did the man do?" SL: The only logical thing to do. He pulled down his trousers." SM: "Oh, no! What happened then?" SL: "Isn't it logical, Sister? A nun with her dress up can run faster than a man with his trousers down!"

At every tea-break, Sean, the hod-carrier was always boasting to his older work-mate, Mike the brick- layer, that he was the better worker because he was stronger, faster, and younger. Mike stoically put up with the bragging until one day, he couldn't take it any more. "Well, Sean", he said, I'll bet a week's wages I can haul something in a wheelbarrow over to that building that you won't be able to wheel back." Sean laughed derisively and agreed to the bet. With that, Mike grabbed the handles of the wheelbarrow and told Sean to get in.

A man and his wife, now in their 60's, were celebrating their 40th wedding anniversary. On their special day, a good fairy came to them and said that because they had been such a devoted couple she would grant each of them a very special wish. The wife wished for a trip around the world with her husband. Whoosh! Immediately she had airline & cruise tickets in her hands. The man wished for a female companion, 30 years younger..... Whoosh! Immediately he turned ninety!!!

Katie and Moira are old friends. They have both been married to their husbands for a long time. Katie is upset because she thinks her husband doesn't find her attractive anymore. "As I get older he doesn't bother to look at me!" she complains to Moira. "What a pity," says Moira. As I get older my husband says I get more beautiful every day. "All well and good, says Katie, but your husband's an antique dealer!"

The concierge at a posh resort was often asked about the ski facilities. One day a couple who had just checked in after a long flight came by and asked me where the lift was. "Go down the hill," he told them, "out the door, past the pool, 200 yards down the block, and you'll see it on your right." Their tired faces suddenly looked even more exhausted until the man behind them spoke up. "They're from Ireland," he said. "I think they're looking for the elevator."

In Killarney, an American tourist sees a sign in front of a farmhouse: "Talking Dog for Sale." He rings the bell and the farmer tells him the dog is around the back. The tourist goes behind the house and sees a black mutt just sitting there "You talk?" he asks. "Indeed." the dog replies. "So, what's your story?" The mutt looks up and says, "Well, I discovered my gift of talking when I was very young and I wanted to be of help to humanity, so I told Interpol about my gift; in no time they had me flying from country to country, sitting in rooms with world leaders, because no one would believe a dog would be listening. I was one of their most valuable spies for eight years running. The jetting around really tired me out, and I knew I wasn't getting any younger. So I signed up for a job at the airport to do some undercover security work, mostly wandering near suspicious characters and eavesdropping. I uncovered some very shady dealings there and was awarded a ton of medals. Then I settled down, had a wife, a dozen or so puppies, and now I'm just retired." The tourist is amazed. He goes back and asks the farmer what he wants for the dog. The farmer says, "Ten euros, sir." The tourist sputters, "But that dog is incredible. Why on earth are you selling him so cheap?" The farmer shrugs and says "Ah well, sir, you, see, isn't he just the biggest liar this side of Croagh Patrick? He's done none of what he told ye."

Father Doyle was a clever speaker and a firm advocate of abstinence, the closure of pubs on Sundays, and a standard of morality that would ensure a warm welcome in Heaven. One Sunday morning, among his listeners was a young country girl who was new to the parish. She was deeply impressed with the priest's eloquent preaching. Indeed, so impressed that she included a few lines about him in her next letter home:"I never get tired of listening to Father Doyle. He is such a lovely speaker, you'd swear that every word he says is true."

A Catholic priest, a Protestant minister, and a Jewish rabbi were discussing when life begins. "Life begins," said the priest, "at the moment of fertilization. That is when God instills the spark of life into the fetus." "We believe," said the minister, "that life begins at birth, because that is when the baby becomes an individual and is capable of making its own decisions and must learn about sin." "You're both wrong," said the rabbi. "Life begins when the children have graduated and moved out of the house."

Two Irish men are in a plane. The roof comes off! Mick says to Paddy, "If this plane turns upside down will we fall out?" "No way Mick" says Paddy, "we'll still be best friends."

Three priests went for a ramble in the country. It was unusually hot for Ireland in September and before too long, they were sweating profusely. They came upon a small lake and since it was fairly secluded, they took off all their clothes and jumped into the water. Feeling refreshed, the trio decided to pick a few blackberries while enjoying their "freedom". As they were crossing an open area, they saw a group of ladies from the village coming towards them. Unable to get to their clothes in time, two of the priests covered their privates, but the third one covered his face while they ran for cover. After the ladies had left and the men got their clothes back on, the first two priests asked the third why he covered his face rather than his privates. "I don't know about you two," he replied, "but in my parish, it's my face they would recognize."

An Irishman, a Mexican and a blond guy were doing construction work on the roof of a skyscraper. They were eating lunch and the Irishman said, "Corned beef and cabbage. If I get corned beef and cabbage one more time for lunch I'm going to jump off this building." The Mexican opened his lunch box and exclaimed, "Burritos again! If I get burritos one more time I'm going to jump off, too." The blond opened his lunch and said, "Bologna again. If I get a bologna sandwich one more time, I'm jumping as well." The next day the Irishman opened his lunch box, saw corned beef and cabbage and jumped. The Mexican opened his lunch, saw a burrito and jumped. The blond guy opened his lunch, saw the bologna and jumped. At the funeral, the Irishman's wife was weeping. She said, "If I'd known how tired he was of corned beef and cabbage, I never would have given it to him again!" The Mexican's wife also wept and said, "I could have given him tacos or enchiladas! I didn't realize he was so bored with burritos." Everyone turned and stared at the blonde guy's wife... wait for it......... "Hey, don't look at me," she said, "He makes his own lunch."

A Catholic priest and a nun were taking a rare afternoon off and enjoying a round of golf. The priest stepped up to the first tee and took a mighty swing. He missed the ball entirely and said "!*#!, I missed." The good Sister told him to watch his language. On his next swing, he missed again. "!*#!, I missed." "Father, I'm not going to play with you if you keep swearing," the nun said tartly. The priest promised to do better and the round continued. On the 4th tee, he misses again.

The usual comment followed. Sister is really angry now and says, "Father , God is going to strike you dead if you keep swearing like that." On the next tee, Father swings and misses again. "!*#!, I missed." A terrible rumble is heard and a gigantic bolt of lightning comes out of the sky and strikes the nun dead in her tracks. And from the sky comes a booming voice......... "S!*#!, I missed."

The store manager, O'Reilly, heard Maryann his assistant tell a customer, "No mam, we haven't had any for a while, and it doesn't look as if we'll be getting any soon." O'Reilly was horrified and ran over to the customer and said, "Of course we'll have some soon. We placed an order last week." Then he took the assistant aside and said, "Never, never, say we're out of anything - say we've got it on order and it's coming. Now what was it she wanted?" "Rain," said the assistant.

A mother was preparing pancakes for her sons, Kevin, 5, and Ryan, 3. The boys began to squabble over who would get the first pancake. Their mother saw the opportunity for a moral lesson. "If Jesus were sitting here, He would say, 'Let my brother have the first pancake, I can wait.'" Kevin turned to his younger brother and said, "Ryan, you be Jesus!"

Idly, the American tourist watched the Cork man dig and turn over the soil. Eventually he called out: "Hey, buddy, what's that you're doing?" "I'm digging potatoes, sir." "Potatoes? You call those puny things potatoes? Back home in Idaho we have potatoes ten times that size!" "Indeed sir, and that's as it needs be; a good potato should be of a size to fit the mouth."

A dietitian was addressing a large audience in Dublin. “The material we put into our stomachs is enough to have killed most of us sitting here, years ago. Red meat is awful. Soft drinks erode your stomach lining. Chinese food is loaded with MSG. Vegetables can be disastrous, and none of us realizes the long-term harm caused by the germs in our drinking water. But there is one food that is the most dangerous of all and we all have, or will, eat it. Can anyone here tell me what food it is that causes the most grief and suffering for years after eating it?” A 75-year-old man in the front row stood up and said, “Wedding cake.”

A bit of graveyard humor: Beneath this stone lies Murphy. They buried him today. He lived the life of Reilly while Reilly was away

Seamus O’Brien had been hailed as the most intelligent Irish man for three years running. He had topped such shows as Larry Gogans ‘Just a Minute Quiz’ and ‘Quicksilver’. It was suggested by the Irish Mensa board that he should enter into the English Mastermind

Championships. He did, and won a place. On the evening of the competition, Seamus walks on stage, sits down and makes himself comfortable. The lights dim and a spotlight shines on his face. Magnus, the emcee, proceeds: "Seamus, what subject are you studying?" Seamus responds, "Irish history". "Very well," says Magnus, "your first question - in what year did the 'Easter Rising take place?" "Pass," says Seamus. "Okay," says Magnus, "Who was the leader of the Easter Rising?" Seamus responds, "Pass." "Well then," says Magnus, "how long did the Easter Rising last?" Again, Seamus responds, "Pass." Instantly, a voice from the audience shouts out: "Good man, Seamus - tell the English nothing..."

The teacher asked each of her students how they celebrated Christmas. She calls first on young Patrick O'Flaherty. "Tell me, Patrick, what do you do at Christmas time? Patrick addresses the class: "Me and my twelve brothers and sisters go to midnight Mass and we sing carols. Then we come home very late and we hang up our pillowcases at the foot of the bed. Then we go to bed and wait for Father Christmas to come with all our toys."

"Very nice, Patrick," the teacher says. "Now, Billy Murphy, what do you do at Christmas?" "Me and my sister go to church with Mum and Dad, and we also sing carols. When we get home, we put biscuits and milk by the chimney and hang up our stockings. We hardly sleep waiting for Santa Claus to bring our presents." "That's also very nice, Billy," she said. Realizing that there was a Jewish boy in the class and not wanting to leave him out of the discussion, she asked him the same question. "Now, Isaac, what do you do at Christmas?" "Well, we also sing carols," Isaac responds. Surprised, the teacher questions further. "Tell us what you sing." "Well, it's the same thing every year. Dad comes home from the office. We all pile into the Rolls Royce and drive to his toy factory. When we get inside, we look at all the empty shelves and sing, 'What a friend we have in Jesus.' Then we all go to the Bahamas."

A passerby watched two Kerry men in a park. One was digging holes and the other was immediately filling them in again. "Tell me," said the passerby, "What on earth are you doing?" "Well," said the digger, "Usually there are three of us. I dig, Paddy plants the tree and Mick fills in the hole. Today Paddy is off ill, but that doesn't mean Mick and I get the day off, does it?"

Two Irish women walking through the forest one day hear a voice coming from near a log. "Help me." They lifted the log and underneath found a frog. "Help me " said the frog "I am an investment banker turned into a frog by an evil curse. I need to be kissed by a woman and I will turn back into an investment banker." One of the women grabbed the frog and stuffed it into her handbag. Aghast, her friend said, "Did you not hear the frog? He needs to to be returned to being an investment banker." "Listen", her friend said. "these days a talking frog is worth a lot more than an investment banker."

Two English counterfeiters had produced thousands of genuine-looking notes - £50, £20, £10 - and really they should have been happy with their lot. Much wants more, so they scrambled through the discarded notes that had not passed close scrutiny. Among the jumble they came upon a perfectly fine note - watermarked, Queen's head in exactly the right place. The only trouble was that the amount shown was £18. Never mind,' said Brown, the bossman. "We'll unload it when we're over in Ireland." And so they took the note with them and, whilst in Kerry, they entered a corner shop to dispense with it "Excuse me," said Brown to shopkeeper Casey. "Have you got change for an £18 note?" "Indeed, sir," said Casey. "And would you like three sixes or two nines?"

When my wife's sister, Patty, was very young, she was allowed to have her best friend, a boy named Rory, over to spend the night. As the children grew toward adolescence, their parents knew that someday the sleepovers would have to end. One night, when Rory and his family were visiting, everyone gathered around the television to watch the Rose of Tralee pageant. When Patty asked if Rory could stay over, the parents hesitated, wondering if the time had finally come to discontinue the tradition. At that moment, the pageant host announced a contestant's measurements: 36-22-36. "Rory," his mother asked, "what are those numbers?" The boy thought for only a moment before responding, "Ninety-four?"Rory was allowed to stay.

For many years Kate Murphy had run the fruit and vegetable stall in the town market and she'd learned to have an answer for any situation. So there she stood, watching the big Texan who was poking around the stall. 'Hey, what are these?' he asked. 'Apples,' said Kate. 'Apples?' laughed the Yank. 'Why, in Texas we have apples twice that size! And what are these?' "Those are potatoes," said Kate. "Potatoes? Where I come from, bragged the Texan, our potatoes are twice as big at least," Just then he picked up a cabbage, but before he could speak Kate said: "If you're not buying Brussels sprouts, you'd best be putting that down."

Sally was driving home from one of her business trips in Northern Ireland when she saw an elderly woman walking on the side of the road. As the trip was a long and quiet one, she stopped the car and asked the woman if she would like a ride. After a bit of small talk and while resuming the journey the woman noticed a brown bag on the seat next to Sally. What's in the bag?" asked the woman. Sally looked down at the brown bag and said, "It's a bottle of wine, I got it for my husband." The woman was silent for a moment. Then speaking with the quiet wisdom of an elder she said: "Good trade."

A couple had two little boys, ages 8 and 10, who were excessively mischievous. They were always getting into trouble and their parents knew that, if any mischief occurred in their village, their sons were probably involved. The boys' mother heard that the local vicar had been successful in disciplining children, so she asked if he would speak with her boys. The vicar agreed, but asked to see them individually. So the mother sent her 8-year-old in first that morning; with the older boy to see the vicar in the afternoon. The vicar, a huge man with a booming voice, sat the younger boy down and asked him sternly, "Where is God?" The boy's mouth dropped open, but he made no response, sitting there with his mouth hanging open, wide eyed. So the vicar repeated the question in an even sterner tone, "Where is God!!?" Again the boy made no attempt to answer. So the vicar raised his voice even more and shook his finger in the boy's face and bellowed, "WHERE IS GOD!!!!?" The boy screamed and bolted from the room, ran directly home and dived into a cupboard, slamming the door behind him. When his older brother found him in the cupboard, he asked, "What happened?" The younger brother, gasping for breath, replied, "We are in BIG trouble this time. God is missing - and they think WE did it.!"

Sean got home in the early hours of the morning after a night at the local pub. He made such a racket as he weaved his way through the house that he woke up the wife. "By all the saints, what are you doing down there?" she shouted from the bedroom. "Get yourself up here and don't be waking the neighbours." "I'm trying to get a barrel of Guinness up the stairs," he shouted back. "Leave it 'till the morning," she shouted down. "I can't" says he, "I've drank it!"

Old Scotland. Two nearby castles are at war. One shoots a cannonball at the other. Bang. A piece of wall breaks. In a while the second castle shoots at the first one. A part of a tower becomes a pile of stones. And so on for some time. Then there is a long silence. Suddenly from one of the castles a cry is heard: "Why don't you shoot?" And the answer: "You have the cannonball."

A Jesuit priest decided to visit a small island off the coast of Connemara. The inhabitants numbered no more than a couple of dozen, but the priest threw himself into the Lord's work with a vengeance. Having taken over the bar of the pub for Mass, and having delivered a fire and brimstone sermon, he questioned his small congregation. "How long is it since any of you had your confessions heard?" he asked. "Well, Father," answered Brendan, the oldest inhabitant. "It must be three years since the last priest was here." "Why didn't you make a trip to the mainland?" thundered the priest. "Well, Father," said Brendan, "the water between us and the mainland is very rough, and our boat is old and leaky. So you see. if we've only venial sins to confess, it's not worth the bother, and if we've mortal sins, it's not worth the risk!"

A minister dies and is waiting in line at the Pearly Gates. Ahead of him is a lad dressed in sunglasses, loud shirt, leather jacket, and jeans. Saint Peter addresses the lad: "Who are you, so that I may know whether or not to admit you to the Kingdom of Heaven?" The fellah replies, "I'm Johnny O'Rourke, taxi-driver, Brooklyn, New York." Saint Peter consults his list. He smiles and says to the taxi-driver, "Take this silken robe and golden staff and enter the Kingdom of Heaven." The taxi-driver goes into Heaven with his robe and staff, and it's the minister's turn. He stands erect and booms out, "I am Phillip Smith, pastor of Saint Mary's for the last forty-three years." Saint Peter consults his list. He says to the minister, "Take this cotton robe and wooden staff and enter the Kingdom of Heaven." "Just a minute," says the minister. "That man was a taxi-driver and he gets a silken robe and golden staff. How can this be?" "Up here, we work by results," says Saint Peter. "While you preached, people slept; while he drove, people prayed."

An attractive young lady was on a plane arriving from Ireland. She found herself seated next to an elderly priest whom she asked: "Excuse me Father, could I ask a favor?" "Of course my child, What can I do for you?" "Here is the problem I bought myself a new sophisticated vibrating hair remover for which I paid an enormous sum of money. I have really gone over the declaration limits and I am worried that they will confiscate it at customs. Do you think you could hide it under your cassock?" "Of course I could, my child, but you must realize that I cannot lie." "You have such an honest face Father, I am sure they will not ask you any questions", and she gave him the worrisome personal gadget. The aircraft arrived at its destination. When the priest presented himself to customs he was asked, "Father, do you have anything to declare?" "From the top of my head to my sash, I have nothing to declare, my son", he replied. Finding his reply strange, the customs officer asked, "And from the sash down, what do you have?" The priest replied, "I have there a marvelous little instrument destined for use by women, but which has never been used." Breaking out in laughter, the customs officer said, "Go ahead Father. Next!"

A minister was completing a temperance sermon. With great emphasis he said, "If I had all the beer in the world, I'd take it and pour it into the river." With even greater emphasis he said, "And if I had all the wine in the world, I'd take it and pour it into the river." And then finally, shaking his fist in the air, he said, "And if I had all the whiskey in the world, I'd take it and pour it into the river." Sermon complete, he then sat down. The choir director stood very cautiously and announced with a smile, for our closing selection, let us sing Hymn #365, "Shall We Gather at the River."

A bit of a groaner, but it made us grin...hope it does the same for you. A party of tourists was taking in the sights on the west coast of Ireland. Having driven for a couple of hours, the coach pulled up at a monastery where the holy hospitalers had prepared tea and cakes. After the snack, the tourists were being shown around the historic building. Entering the kitchen they found a brother slicing potatoes and dropping them into a pan of boiling fat. "Oh I see," said a smart-alec Englishman, "you're obviously a chipmunk?" "No," was the reply, "I'm the friar."

The wife had invited a houseful to Thanksgiving dinner. At the table, she turned to her six-year-old daughter and said, "Would you like to say the blessing?" "I wouldn't know what to say," the girl replied. "Just say what you hear your mother say," the father suggested. The daughter bowed her head and said, "Dear Lord, why on earth did I invite all these people to dinner?"

A young man named Sean received a parrot as a gift. The parrot had a bad attitude and an even worse vocabulary. Every word out of the bird's mouth was rude, obnoxious and even profane. Sean tried and tried to change the bird's attitude by consistently saying only polite words, playing soft music and even reading him Scripture, or anything else he could think of to 'clean up' the bird's vocabulary. Finally, Sean got really fed up and he yelled at the parrot. The parrot just yelled back. Sean shook the parrot and the parrot got angrier and even ruder. In desperation, Sean threw up his hands, grabbed the bird and stuck him in the freezer. For a few minutes the parrot squawked and kicked and screamed. Then suddenly there was total quiet. Not a peep was heard for over a minute. Fearing that he might have really hurt the parrot, Sean quickly opened the door to the freezer. The parrot calmly stepped out onto John's outstretched arms and said, "I believe I may have offended you with my rude, obnoxious language and actions. I'm sincerely remorseful for my inappropriate transgressions and I fully intend to do everything I can to correct my crude and unforgivable behavior." Sean was stunned at the complete change in the bird's attitude! As he was about to ask the parrot what had made such a dramatic change in his behavior, the bird continued, "May I inquire as to what the turkey did?"

It was England v. Ireland at Wembley. It was at that very match when the two Clancy brothers approached the turnstile. "How much is it?" asked Michael "Twenty pounds." said the ticket-seller. "Well, I've only got one eye and so I'm only paying ten!" And, wonder of wonders, the man let him in. "And I'm only paying ten pounds." said Owen. "Hang on," said the ticket seller, "you've got two eyes!" "Yes," said Owen, "but I've only come to see Ireland."

An Irishman sees a job advert published on a building site, 'handymanwanted apply within'. So he does and speaks to the foreman.Foreman: "Can you drive a forklift truck?" Irishman: "No" Foreman: "Can you plaster?" Irishman: "No" Foreman: "Can you brick lay?" Irishman: "No" Foreman: "If you don't mind me asking, what's handy about you?" Irishman: "I only live five minutes down the road."

For 50 years, Paddy left the box alone, until his wife Moira was old and dying. One day, when he was putting their affairs in order, he found the box again and thought it might hold something important. Opening it, he found two doilies and 82,500 pounds in cash. He took the box to her and asked about the contents. “My mother gave me that box the day we married,” she explained. “She told me to make a doily to help ease my frustrations every time I got angry with you.” Paddy was very touched that in 50 years she’d only been vexed with him twice.” What’s the money for?” he asked. “Oh, well that’s what I’ve made selling the Doilies.”

A priest parked his car in a no-parking zone because he was short of time and couldn’t find a space with a meter. Then he put a note under the windshield wiper that read: “I have circled the block 10 times. If I don’t park here, I’ll miss my appointment. Forgive us our trespasses.” When he returned, he found a citation from a police officer along with this note. “I’ve circled this block for 10 years. If I don’t give you a ticket, I’ll lose my job. Lead us not into temptation.”

The wise old Mother Superior from county Tipperary was dying. The nuns gathered around her bed trying to make her comfortable. They gave her some warm milk to drink, but she refused it. Then one nun took the glass back to the kitchen. Remembering a bottle of Irish whiskey received as a gift the previous Christmas, she opened and poured a generous amount into the warm milk. Back at Mother Superior's bed, she held the glass to her lips. Mother drank a little, then a little more. Before they knew it, she had drunk the whole glass down to the last drop. Mother," the nuns asked with earnest, "Please give us some wisdom before you leave us." She raised herself up in bed with a pious look on her face and said, "Don't sell that cow."

A senior citizen in Galway bought a convertible. He took off down the Bishop Connell Road, flooring it to 80 mph and enjoying the wind blowing through what little hair he had left on his head. Then he looked in his rear view mirror and saw a two-bulb behind him. "I can get away from him" thought the old man and he tromped it some more and flew down the road at over 100 mph. Then 110, 120 mph. Then he thought, What am doing? I'm too old to be making such a holy show of meself. He pulled over to the side of the road and waited for the garda to catch up with him. The garda pulled in behind the ole fella and walked up to him. "Sir," he said, looking at his watch. "My shift ends in 30 minutes and today is Friday. If you can give me a reason why you were speeding that I've never heard before, I'll let you go." The man looked at the garda and said, "Years ago my wife ran off with a Peeler and I thought you were bringing her back." "Have a good day, Sir," said the officer.

A lady is having a bad day at the roulette tables. She's down to her last 50 Euros. Exasperated, she exclaims, "What rotten luck I've had today! What in the world should I do now?" A man standing next to her suggests, "I don't know... why don't you play your age?" He walks away. Moments later, his attention is grabbed by a great commotion at the roulette table. Maybe she won! He rushes back to the table and pushes his way through the crowd. The lady is lying limp on the floor, with the table operator kneeling over her. The man is stunned. He asks, "What happened? Is she all right?" The operator replies, "I don't know. She put all her money on 29 and 36 came up. Then she just fainted!"

A man comes home from an exhausting day at work, plops down on the couch in front of the television, and tells his wife, "Get me a Guinness before it starts." The wife sighs and gets him a Guinness. Fifteen minutes later, he says, "Get me another before it starts." She looks cross, but fetches another Guinness and slams it down next to him. He finishes that one and a few minutes later says, "Quick, get me another, it's going to start any minute." The wife is furious. She yells at him "Is that all you're going to do tonight? Drink beer and sit in front of that TV? You're nothing but a diabolical, desperate, mangled midden, and furthermore ..." The man sighs and says, "It's started ..."

The elderly priest, speaking to the younger priest, said, "It was a good idea to replace the first four pews with plush bucket theatre seats. It worked. The front of the chapel fills first." The young priest nodded and the old priest continued, "And you told me a little more beat to the music would bring young people back to Sunday Mass, so I supported you when you brought that rock'n roll gospel choir. We are packed to the balcony." Thank you Father," answered the young priest. "I am pleased you are open to the new ideas of youth." "Well," said the elderly priest. "I'm afraid you've gone too far with the drive-through confessional." "But Father," protested the young priest "My confessions have nearly doubled since I began that!" "I know son," replied the older priest. "But that flashing neon sign, "Toot 'n Tell or Go to Hell," can't stay on the chapel roof!"

A young man from America went to visit his 90-year old grandfather who lived in a very secluded, rural part of Ireland. After his first night, his grandfather prepared a traditional Irish breakfast consisting of eggs, bacon and black pudding.The young man noticed a filmy substance on his plate and he asked his grandfather: "Are these plates clean?" His grandfather replied: "Those plates are as clean as cold water can get them, so go on now and finish your meal." Later in the day, while eating the sandwich his grandfather had made for lunch, the young man noticed tiny specks around the edge of his plate, and what looked like dried egg yolks. So he asked again: "Are you sure these plates are clean?" Without looking up from his sandwich, the grandfather says: “I told you before, those dishes are as clean as cold water can get them - stop being so fussy -you’re in Ireland now, not back in America!” That afternoon, the young man was on his way out to the pub in a nearby village. As he was leaving, his grandfather’s dog started to growl and would not let him pass. “Granddad,” the young man called, “your dog won’t let me out.” Without diverting his attention from the newspaper he was reading, his grandfather shouted: “COLDWATER, get out of the way!”

An old man in Dublin calls his son in New York right before Christmas and says, “Son, I ‘m sorry, but I have to tell you that after 45 years of misery, your mother and I are busting up.” “Da, what are you talking about?” the son yells in disbelief. “We can’t stand the sight of each other any longer,” the father says. “We’re sick of each other, and I’m sick of talking about this, so you call your sister in Chicago and tell her.” Frantic, the son calls his sister, who explodes on the phone. “No way they’re leaving each other!” she shouts, “I’ll take care of this.” She calls Dublin immediately and screams at her father, “You are not splitting up. Don’t do a single thing until I get there. I'm calling my brother back, and we'll both be there tomorrow. Until then, don't do a thing, DO YOU HEAR ME?" and hangs up. The old man hangs up his phone and turns to his wife. "Well then," he says, "they're coming home for Christmas and paying their own way!"

Seamus was getting exasperated and shouted upstairs to his wife," Sheila, will you please hurry up or we'll be late. "Oh, calm yourself, Seamus" Sheila replied. "Haven't I been telling you for the last hour that I'll be ready in a minute?"

Sean goes into his dentist's office, because of a pain in his mouth. After a brief examination, the dentist exclaims, "Good God, man! That plate I installed in your mouth about six months ago has nearly completely corroded! What on earth have you been eating?" "Well... the only thing I can think of is this... my wife made me some asparagus about four months ago with this stuff on it...Hollandaise sauce she called it... and doctor, I'm talking' DELICIOUS! I've never tasted anything like it, and ever since then I've been putting it on everything...meat, fish, toast, vegetables...everything." "That's probably it," replied the dentist "Hollandaise sauce is made with lemon juice, which is acidic and highly corrosive. It seems as though I'll have to install a new plate, but made out of chrome this time." "Why chrome?" Sean asked. "Well," said the dentist, "everyone knows that there's no plate like chrome for the Hollandaise."

Mrs. Casey was telling her friend Mrs. Kelly about a rather juicy rumour. "That's very interesting," said Mrs. Kelly. "Come on, tell me more about it." Mrs. Casey said, "I can't. I've already told you more than I heard!"

A man and his wife are awakened at 3 o'clock in the morning by a loud pounding on the door. The man gets up and goes to the door; when he opens it, an obviously inebriated stranger is standing there in the pouring rain. The stranger asks for a push. "Jam on your egg," says the husband, "it's three o'clock in the morning!" He slams the door and goes back to bed. "Who was that?" asked his wife.

"Just some fluthered eejit asking for a push," he answers. "Did you help him?" she asks. "No, I did not, it's three in the morning and it's lashing out there." "Well, you have a short memory," says his wife. "Remember about three months ago when we broke down and that nice couple helped us out? I think you should help him; you should be ashamed of yourself!" The man sighs, does as he is told, gets dressed, and goes out into the pouring rain. He calls out into the dark, "Hello, are you still there?" "Yes," comes back the answer. "Do you still need a push?" calls out the husband. "Yes, please!" comes the reply from the dark. "Where are you?" asks the husband. "Over here, on the swing!"
*Irish slang: Jam on your egg - wishful thinking; will never happen.

Making Money for the Church Father Murphy was a priest in a very poor parish and asked for suggestions as to how he could raise money for the church. He was told that the horse owner always had money, so he went to the horse auction, but made a very poor buy, as the horse turned out to be a donkey. However, he thought he might as well enter the donkey in a race. The donkey came in third, and the next morning, the headlines in the paper read: FATHER MURPHY'S ASS SHOWS The Archbishop saw the paper and was greatly displeased. The next day, the donkey came in first and the headlines read: FATHER MURPHY'S ASS OUT IN FRONT The Archbishop was up in arms. Something had to be done. Father Murphy had entered the donkey again and it had come in second. The headlines read. FATHER MURPHY'S ASS BACK IN PLACE This was too much for the Archbishop, so he forbade the priest to enter the donkey in any more races. The headlines then read: ARCHBISHOP SCRATCHES FATHER MURPHY'S ASS Finally, the Archbishop ordered Father Murphy to get rid of the donkey. He was unable to sell it, so he gave it to Sister Agatha for a pet. The Archbishop ordered her to dispose of the animal at once. She sold it for ten dollars. Next day, the headlines read: SISTER AGATHA PEDDLES ASS FOR TEN DOLLARS They buried the Archbishop three days later.

A group of Kerry engineers is trying to calculate the height of a flag pole. They try to measure its height by lining up their thumbs and then turning the thumb 90 degrees and marking a spot on the ground. Then they try to use its shadow and trig functions, but no luck. An engineer from Dublin comes by and watches for a few minutes. He asks one of the Kerry engineers what they're doing. "We're trying to calculate the height of this flag pole." The Dublin engineer watches a few minutes more and then, without saying a word, he walks over, pulls the pole out of the ground, lays it down, measures it, writes the measurement on a piece of paper, gives it to one of the Kerry group. The Kerry man looks at the paper, snickers and says to the others: "Isn't that just like a Dubliner? We're trying to calculate the height and he gives us the length."

An elderly looking gentleman, (mid nineties) very well dressed, hair well groomed, great looking suit, flower in his lapel, smelling slightly of a good after shave, presenting a well-looked-after image, walks into an upscale cocktail lounge in Dublin. Seated at the bar is an elderly looking lady, (mid eighties). The gentleman walks over, sits along side of her, orders a drink, takes a sip, turns to her and says, "So tell me, do I come here often?"

Alice was to bake a cake for the church ladies' group bake sale, but she forgot to do it until the last minute. She baked an angel food cake and when she took it from the oven, the center had dropped flat. She said, "Oh dear, there's no time to bake another cake." So, she looked around the house for something to build up the center of the cake. Alice found it in the bathroom ... a roll of toilet paper. She plunked it in and covered it with icing. The finished product looked beautiful, so she rushed it to the church. Before she left the house, Alice had given her daughter some money and specific instructions to be at the bake sale the minute it opened, and to buy that cake and bring it home. When the daughter arrived at the sale, the attractive cake had already been sold. Alice was beside herself. The next day, Alice was invited to a friend's home where two tables of bridge were to be played that afternoon. Before the game, a fancy lunch was served, and to top it off, the cake in question was presented for dessert. Alice saw the cake, she started to get out of her chair to rush into the kitchen to tell her hostess all about it, but before she could get to her feet, one of the other ladies said, "What a beautiful cake!" Alice sat back in her chair when she heard the hostess (who was a prominent church member) say, "Thank you, I baked it myself."

I was on the 7.45 a.m bus over thirty years ago, one miserable monday morning on the way to work after catching the first bus half an hour earlier which brought me in to O'Connell Bridge in Dublin through the torrents of rain to get on this one soaking wet. Well upstairs (which was in those days the smoking deck, as you might remember), I sat down next to a window and looked out the window only to see the darkness of another horrible early morning traffic jam with the cars and lorries all trying to get out of Dublin.

I was training to be a watchmaker out in Blanchardstown. Anyhow with the rain pouring down and the heavy pall of cigarette smoke hanging over the packed upper level of the C.I.E bus you could hear a pin drop as everybody was thoroughly dejected at another dismal trip out to, as Americans would call it, "The Boonies". You could also see the steam rising off the occupants of the bus as the heater at full blast was now drying out some of the passengers who had been on the longest. Which made you at least realize, you were actually better off on the bus than trudging through the rain to wherever you needed to go! Well as I said it was extremely quiet and all that could be heard were the smokers exhaling into this growing fog. There were two Country fellas as we would call them in Dublin behind me and one said to the other, "Mick, were you at the match in Croke park yesterday?" Mick said just a flat "No" and the other fella whose name heard was Brendan said, "all the fellas in his work thought that people who liked hurling were proper eejits!". There was silence for the next 30 seconds or so until Mick said matter of factly, "Isn't it gas all the same Brendan, how they can get 80,000 eejits at one time in the one place." I laughed all the way out to Blanchardstown. over 45 minutes - Mind you not too loud, they were also bigger than me at the time.

The local priest had just hired a new housekeeper, Mary. The first morning while Father was having breakfast, Mary entered the room and exclaimed that the toaster was not working. He explained to Mary now that she was part of the household she should refer to the toaster as "our toaster". A few days later Mary mentioned to Father that the refrigerator was not working. He once again explained that she should refer to it as "our refrigerator". About a month later, the priest was entertaining the Bishop for dinner when Mary rushed into the room screaming in panic, "Father, Father, there's a mouse under our bed!"

Sarah and her thirteen-year-old sister had been fighting a lot this year. This happens when you combine a headstrong four-year-old, who is sure she is always right, with a young adolescent. Sarah's parents, trying to take advantage of her avid interest in what Santa might bring, reminded the four-year-old that Santa was watching and doesn't like it when children fight. This had little impact."I'll just have to tell Santa about your misbehavior," the mother said as she picked up the phone and dialed. Sarah's eyes grew big as her mother asked "Mrs. Claus" (Sarah's aunt), if she could put Santa on the line. Sarah's mouth dropped open as Mom described to Santa (Sarah's uncle) how the four-year-old was acting. But, when Mom said that Santa wanted to talk to her, she reluctantly took the phone. Santa, in a deepened voice, explained to her how there would be no presents Christmas morning to children who fought with their sisters. He would be watching, and he expected things to be better from now on. Sarah, now even more wide eyed, solemnly nodded to each of Santa's remarks and silently hung the phone up when he was done. After a long moment, Mom (holding in her chuckles at being so clever) asked, "What did Santa say to you, sweetie?" In almost a whisper, Sarah sadly but matter-of-factly stated, "Santa said he won't be bringing toys to my sister this year."

Father O'Malley was going through the post one day. Drawing a single sheet of paper from an envelope, he found written on it just one word: “FOOL.” The next Sunday at Mass, he announced, “I have known many people who have written letters and forgot to sign their names. But this week I received a letter from someone who signed their name and forgot to write a letter.”

It was opening night at the theatre and The Amazing Claude was topping the bill. People came from miles around to see the famous hypnotist do his stuff. As Claude took to the stage, he announced, “Unlike most stage hypnotists, who invite two or three people up onto the stage to be put into a trance, I intend to hypnotize each and every member of the audience. “The excitement was almost electric as Claude withdrew a beautiful antique pocket watch from his coat. “I want you each to keep your eye on this antique watch. It’s a very special watch. It’s been in my family for six generations.” He began to swing the watch gently back and forth while quietly chanting, “Watch the watch, watch the watch, watch the watch...” The crowd became mesmerized as the watch swayed back and forth, light gleaming off it’s polished surface. Hundreds of pairs of eyes followed the swaying watch, until suddenly it slipped from the hypnotist's fingers and fell to the floor, breaking into a hundred pieces! "S***"! yelled Claude. It took three weeks to clean up the theatre.

At 85 years of age, Patrick marries Kate, a lovely 25 year old. Since her new husband is getting on in years, Kate decides that after their wedding she and Patrick should have separate bedrooms, because she is concerned that he might overexert himself if they spend the entire night together. After the wedding festivities Kate prepares herself for bed and the expected "knock" on the door. Sure enough the knock comes, the door opens and there is Patrick, her 85 year old groom, ready to make love. They unite as one. All goes well, Patrick takes leave of his bride, and she prepares to go to sleep. After a few minutes, Kate hears another knock on her bedroom door, and it's Patrick. Again he is ready for more love-making. Somewhat surprised, Kate consents. When the newlyweds are done, Patrick kisses his bride, bids her a fond goodnight and leaves. She is set to go to sleep again, but, aha you guessed it - Patrick is back, rapping on the door, and is as fresh as a 25-year-old. Once more. they enjoy each other. But as Patrick gets set to leave again, his young bride says to him, “I am thoroughly impressed that at 85 you can perform so well and so often. I have heard that most men a third of your age are only any good just once. You are truly a great lover, Patrick.” Patrick, somewhat embarrassed, turns to Kate and says: “You mean I was here already?”

Father Guffy roared from the pulpit to his | parishioners: “The drink has killed millions - it rots their stomachs and they die in agony. Smoking has killed millions - it coats your lungs and you die in agony. Overeating and consorting with loose women have also killed millions...”” ‘Scuse me, Father,” hollered Reagan from the back, “but what is it that kills the people who live right?”

Sean met a woman at a luxurious resort and fell head over heels in love with her. On the last night the two of them went to dinner and had a serious talk about how they would continue the relationship. Sean began by saying to his new lady friend that while she meant a lot to him, “It’s only fair to warn you that when I'm at home I am completely consumed by golf. I eat, sleep and breath golf. so if that's a problem, you'd better say so right now." "Well, since we're being honest with each other, here goes," she replied."I'm a hooker." "I see," replied Sean, and was quiet for a moment. Then he added, "You know, it's probably because you're not keeping your wrists straight when you tee off."

Father O'Malley arose one fine spring morning, walked to the window of his bedroom to take in the beauty of the day and noticed there was a jackass lying dead in the middle of his front lawn. He promptly called the gardai. The conversation went like this: "Dia Dhuit, this is Sgt. O' Flaherty and how might we be of help to you?" "Good day to yourself, Sergeant. This is Father O'Malley at St. Brigid's. There's a jackass lying dead on our front lawn. Would you be a good man now and send a couple of the lads to to take care of the matter?" Sgt. Flaherty considered himself to be quite a wit and the rest of the conversation proceeded: "Well now, Father, it was always my impression that you took care of the last rites!" There was dead silence on the line for a moment and then Father O'Malley replied: "Indeed, indeed, Sergeant O'Flaherty, but we're also obliged to notify the next of kin!"

Sean and his wife, Aoife, had been debating buying a vehicle for weeks. He wanted a truck. She wanted a fast little sports-like car so she could zip through traffic around town. He would probably have settled on any beat up old truck, but everything she seemed to like was way out of their price range. "Look!" she said. "I want something that goes from 0 to 200 in just a few seconds. Nothing else will do. My birthday is coming up so surprise me!" Sean did just that. For her birthday, he bought her a brand new bathroom scale. Nobody has seen or heard from him since.

A farmer finally decided to buy a TV. The store assured him that they would install the antenna and TV the next day.The next evening the farmer turned on his new TV and found only political adverts on every channel. The next morning he turned the TV on and found only political adverts again. When he came in to eat dinner he tried the TV again but still only found political adverts. The next day when he still found only political adverts he called the store to complain. The owner said that it was impossible for every channel to only have political adverts, but agreed to send their repairman to check the TV. When the TV repairman turned on the TV he found that the farmer was right. After looking at the TV for a while he went outside to check the antenna. In a few minutes he returned and told the farmer he had found the problem. The antenna had been installed on top of the windmill and grounded to the manure spreader.

A European tourist is lost and stops in an Irish village to ask for directions. He sees two old men sitting outside the pub enjoying their Guinness. “Parlez-vous Francais, he asks. The old men look at each other and shake their heads. “Sprechen sie Deutsch?” Again, the old men shake their heads. Beginning to get a bit irritated, the tourist asks “Habla Espanol?” The men once again shake their heads. Totally exasperated by now, the tourist asks “Parla l’italiano?” The men once again look at each other and then shake their heads in puzzlement. The tourist is so disgusted that he drives off. One old man says to the other, “You know, Sean, perhaps we should learn another language.” “Ah get on with yeh; look at him, he knows four and it didn’t do him a bit of good.”

A Sunday School teacher decided to have her young class memorize one of the most quoted passages in the Bible; Psalm 23. She gave the youngsters a month to learn the verse. Little Sean was excited about the task. But, he just couldn't remember the Psalm. After much practice, he could barely get past the first line. On the day that the kids were scheduled to recite Psalm 23 in front of the congregation, Sean was so nervous that when it was his turn, he stepped up to the microphone and said proudly, "The Lord is my shepherd and that's all I need to know."

Brendan was driving down the street in a sweat because he had an important meeting and couldn't find a parking place. Looking up to heaven he said, "Lord take pity on me. If you find me a parking place I will go to Mass every Sunday for the rest of me life and give up the drink." Miraculously, a parking place appeared. Brendan looked up again and said, "Never mind, I found one."

Father Murphy was playing golf with a parishioner. On the first hole, he sliced into the rough. His opponent heard him mutter "Hoover!" under his breath. On the second hole, the ball went straight into a water hazard. "Hoover!" again, a little louder this time. On the third hole, a miracle occurred and Fr. Murphy's drive landed on the green only six inches from the hole! "Praise be to God!" He carefully lined up the putt, but the ball curved around the hole instead of going in. "HOOVER!" By this time, his opponent couldn't withhold his curiosity any longer, and asked why the priest said 'Hoover'. "It's the biggest dam I know," said the priest.

A couple goes for a meal at a Chinese restaurant and orders the "Chicken Surprise." The waiter brings the meal, served in a lidded cast-iron pot. Just as the wife is about to serve herself, the lid of the pot rises slightly and she briefly sees two beady little eyes looking around before the lid slams back down. "Good grief, did you see that?" she asks her husband. He hasn't, so she asks him to look in the pot. He reaches for it and again the lid rises, and he sees two little eyes looking around before it slams down. Sputtering in a fit of pique, he calls the waiter over, describes what is happening, and demands an explanation! "Please sir," says the waiter, "what you order?" The husband replies, "Chicken Surprise." "Ah... so sorry," says the waiter, "I bring you Peeking Duck."

Paddy and Mick had emigrated from Ireland and worked together in an Ontario clothing factory. Both were laid off, so they went to the unemployment office. When asked his occupation, Paddy answered, 'panty stitcher'. I sews the lastic onta ladies' cotton knickers. The clerk looked up 'panty stitcher' on his computer and finding it classified as unskilled labour, he gave Paddy $80 dollars a week unemployment pay. Mick was next in and when asked his occupation, he replied, 'diesel fitter'. Since 'diesel fitter' was a skilled job, the clerk gave Mick $160 dollars a week. When Paddy found out, he was furious. He stormed back into the office to find out why his friend and co-worker was collecting double his pay. The clerk explained, 'panty stitchers' are unskilled and 'diesel fitters' are skilled labour. "What skill?" yelled Paddy?! "I sews da lastic onta da knickers. Mick puts dem over his head and says: 'Right ye are so, dese ‘ull fit her.’”

Three sons left home, went out on their own and prospered. Getting back together, they discussed the gifts they were able to give their elderly mother. The first said, “I built a big house for our mother.” The second said,” I sent her a BMW with a driver.” The third smiled and said, “I’ve got you, both beat. You know how Mom enjoys the Bible, and you know she can’t see very well. I sent her a parrot that can recite the entire Bible. It took 20 monks in an Irish monastery 12 years to teach him. I had to pledge to contribute $100,000.00 a year for 10 years, but it was worth it. Mom just has to name the chapter and verse, and the parrot will recite it.”Soon thereafter, Mom sent out her letters of thanks: “ “Seamus,” she wrote the first son, “the house you built is so huge. I live in only one room, but I have to clean the whole house.” “Sean,” she wrote to another, “I am too old to travel. I stay home all the time, so I never use the BMW. And the driver is so rude!” “Dearest Donal,” she wrote to her third son, “You were the only son to have the good sense to know what your mother likes. That chicken was delicious.”

A guy sitting at a bar in an international airport noticed a very beautiful woman sitting next to him. He thought to himself, “Wow, she’s so gorgeous she must be a flight attendant. But which airline does she work for? Hoping to pick her up, he leaned towards her and uttered the Delta slogan: “Love to fly and it shows?” She gave him a blank, confused stare and he immediately thought to himself, “Oh darn, she doesn’t work for Delta”. A moment later, another slogan popped into his head. He leaned towards her again, “Something special in the air?” She gave him the same confused look. He mentally kicked himself, and scratched Singapore Airlines off the list. Next he tried the Thai Airways slogan: “Smooth as Silk.” This time the woman turned on him “What in God’s name do you want?” The man smiled, then slumped back in his chair, and said, “Ahhhhh, Aer Lingus!”

A furniture dealer from Kerry decided that he wanted to expand the line of furniture in his store, so he decided to go to Paris, France to see what he could find. After arriving in Paris (this being his first trip ever to the French capitol), he met with some manufacturers and finally selected a line that he thought would sell well back home in Kerry. To celebrate the new acquisition, he decided to visit a small bistro and have a glass of wine. As he sat enjoying his wine, he noticed that the small place was quite crowded, and that the one other chair at his table was the only vacant seat in the house. Before long, a very beautiful young Parisian girl came to his table, asked him something in French (which he did not understand), and motioned toward the chair. He invited her to sit down. He tried to speak to her in English, but she did not speak his language so, after a couple of minutes of trying to communicate with her, he took a napkin and drew a picture of a wine glass and showed it to her. She nodded, and he ordered a glass of wine for her. After sitting together at the table for awhile, he took another napkin, and drew a picture of a plate with food on it, and she nodded. They left the bistro and found a quiet cafe that featured a small group playing romantic music. They ordered dinner, after which he took another napkin and drew a picture of a couple dancing. She nodded, and they got up to dance. They danced until the cafe closed and the band was packing up. Back at their table, the young lady took a napkin and drew a picture of a four-poster bed. To this day, he has no idea how she figured out he was in the furniture business.

Two Kerry factory workers were talking. "I think I'll take some time off from work." said the man. "How do you think you'll do that?" asked the blonde. He proceeded to climb up to the rafters and hung from them upside down. His supervisor walked in, saw the worker hanging from the ceiling, and asked him what on earth he was doing. "I'm a light bulb," answered the man. "I think you need some time off," said the supervisor. So, the man jumped down and walked out of the factory. The blonde began walking out too. "Where do you think you're going?" demanded the supervisor. The blonde answered, "Home, sir. I can't work in the dark."

The Doctor was puzzled "I'm very sorry but I can't diagnose your trouble, Mahoney. I think it must be drink." "Don't worry about it Dr. Kelley, I'll come back when you're sober."

The American had been fishing for two weeks at Ballinahinch without getting a bite. On the last day of his vacation he caught a small salmon. “Turlough,” he said to his gillie as the fish was gaffed, “that salmon cost me five hundred dollars.” “Well now sir,” comforted Turlough, “aren’t you the lucky man you didn’t catch two.” Sean says to Dr. Flynn, “Doctor, doctor, I can’t stop singing The Green, Green Grass of Home.” “Hmm”, says Dr. Flynn- “That sounds like Tom Jones syndrome.””Is it common?” asks Sean.”It’s not unusual.”

Mr. Smith was travelling through Europe. When he visited the Pope, he noticed a red phone on a small table in the corner of the office. After several minutes of conversation, Smith asked the Pope what the red phone was for. The Holy Father told him that it was a very special phone with a direct line to God. However, the Pope told Smith that he rarely used it because it cost $20,000 a minute from the Vatican. Without another thought, Smith accepted this explanation. Later, when Smith visited Ireland, he saw another red phone in the Archbishop’s office. Being curious, Smith asked the Archbishop what it was for. The Archbishop told Smith it was a direct line to God, and he used it whenever he had a puzzling question or concern. Smith asked if the calls were quite expensive since the Pope had to pay $20,000 a minute when he used his red phone in the Vatican. "Oh no," replied the Archbishop, "In Ireland it's a local call."

A Kerryman gets on a bus and asks the driver how long the trip is between Limerick to Cork. "About 2 hours," says the driver. "Okay," says the Kerryman "then how long is the trip between Cork to Limerick?" The irate driver says "It's still about 2 hours, boyo. Why'd ye think there'd be a difference?" "Well," says the Kerryman, "It's only a week between Christmas and New Year's, but it's a helluva long time between New Year's to Christmas!"

Brothers Mike and Seamus O'Malley were the two richest men in town, and they were also the meanest. They swindled the Church out of its property, foreclosed on the orphanage and cheated widows out of their last mite. And that was just for starters. Finally Seamus up and dies, and Mike pays a visit to the priest. “Father,” he says, “my good name will be upheld in this town. You’ll be givin’ the eulogy for me brother, and in that eulogy you are going to say “Seamus O’Malley was truly a saint.””I won’t do such a thing. T’would be a lie!” “I know you will,” says Mike. “I hold the mortgage on the parish school, and if you don’t say those words, I’ll foreclose.” The priest is over a barrel. “And if I pledge to say those words, then you’ll sign the note over free and clear?” “Done,” cackles Mike, and he signs over the note. Next morning at the funeral, the priest begins the eulogy: “Seamus O’Malley was a mean-spirited, spiteful, penurious, lying, cheating, arrogant and hateful excuse for a human being. But compared to his brother, Mike, Seamus O’Malley was truly a saint.”

A local priest and pastor stood by the side of the road holding up a sign that said, "The End is Near! Turn yourself around now before it'stoo late!" They planned to hold up the sign to each passing car. "Leave us alone, you religious nuts!" yelled the first driver as he sped by. From around the curve they heard a big splash. "Do you think," said one clergy to the other, "we should just put up a sign that says 'bridge out' instead?"

Sister Mary Katherine entered the Convent of Silence. The Mother Superior said, "Sister, you are welcome here as long as you like, but you may not speak until I direct you to do so". Sister Mary Katherine lived in the convent for 5 years before the Mother Superior said to her, "Sister Mary Katherine, you have been here for 5 years. You may speak two words."Sister Mary Katherine said, "Hard bed." "I'm sorry to hear that. We will get you a better bed."After another 5 years, Sister Mary Katherine was called by the Mother Superior. "You may say another two words, Sister Mary Katherine." "Cold food," said Sister Mary Katherine, and the Mother Superior assured her that the food would be better in the future. On her 15th anniversary in the community, the Mother Superior again called Sister Mary Katherine into her office. “You may say two words today.” “I quit,” said Sister Mary Katherine. “It’s probably best”, said the Mother Superior. “You’ve done nothing but gripe since you got here.”

The teacher was explaining the different sizes of whales to her seven year olds, when little Sean raised his hand. “Yes, Sean?” “Teacher! Jonah was swallowed by a whale.” “I don’t think so Sean, a whale doesn’t have a mouth big enough to swallow a man.” “Yes, they do, my bible says so. Jonah was swallowed by a whale.” “Sorry Sean I just cannot believe that.” “Well, when I go to heaven, I’ll ask Jonah.” The teacher replied with a smug grin. “What if Jonah isn’t in heaven Sean?” Sean hesitated for a moment then answered. “Then you can ask him.”

A young girl came to the late Father Healy of Cork, and sadly made her confession: “Father, I fear I’ve committed the sin of vanity,” she announced. “What makes you think that?” asked her father-confessor. “Because every morning, when I look in the mirror, I cannot help but think how beautiful I am." "Never fear, colleen," was the reassuring reply. "That isn't a sin; it's only a mistake."

Four men were bragging about how smart their dogs were. One man was an engineer, the second man was an accountant, the third man was a chemist, and the fourth was a government worker. To show off, the engineer called to his dog. "T-square,do your stuff." T-square trotted over to a desk, took out some paper and a pen, and promptly drew a circle, a square, and a triangle. Everyone agreed that that was quite clever. The accountant said that his dog could do better. He called to his dog and said, "Spreadsheet, do your stuff." Spreadsheet went out into the kitchen and returned with a dozen cookies. He divided them into four equal piles of three cookies each. Everyone agreed that that was good. The chemist said that his dog could do better still. He called to his dog and said, "Measure, do your stuff." Measure got up, walked over to the fridge, took out a quart of milk, got a ten-ounce glass from the cupboard and poured exactly eight ounces without spilling a drop. Everyone agreed that that was very impressive. Then the three men turned to the government worker and said, “What can your dog do?” The government worker called to his dog and said, “Coffee Break, do your stuff.” Coffee Break jumped to his feet, ate the cookies, drank the milk, claimed he had injured his back while doing so, filed a grievance report for unsafe working conditions, put in for workers’ compensation, and went home for the rest of the day on sick leave. They all agreed that that was brilliant!

After the Britain Beer Festival in London, all the brewery presidents decided to go out for a beer. The guy from Corona sits down and says, "Hey Senor, I would like the world's best beer, a Corona." The bartender dusts off a bottle from the shelf and gives it to him. The guy from Budweiser says, "I'd like the best beer in the world, give me 'The King Of Beers', a Budweiser." The bartender gives him one. The guy from Coors says, "I'd like the only beer made with Rocky Mountain spring water, give me a Coors." He gets it. The guy from Guinness sits down and says, "Give me a Coke." The bartender is a little taken aback, but gives him what he ordered. The other brewery presidents look over at him and ask "Why aren't you drinking a Guinness?" and the Guinness president replies, "Well, I figured if you guys aren't drinking beer, neither would I."

The American tourist passed by a farm and saw a beautiful horse. Hoping to buy the animal, he said to the farmer: "I think your horse looks pretty good, so I'll give you 500 punts for him." "He doesn't look so good, and he's not for sale," the farmer said. The tourist insisted, "I think he looks just fine and I'll up the price to 1,000 punts. "He doesn't look so good," the farmer said, "but if you want him that much, he's yours." The next day the tourist came back in a rage. He went up to the farmer and screamed, "You sold me a blind horse. You cheated me!" The farmer calmly replied, "Now how could that be. I told you he didn't look so good, didn't I?"

The Monsignor greeted Paddy and said "Congratulations on your 50th wedding anniversary"! Have you any plans made on how to celebrate?""Well," said Paddy, "on our 25th Anniversary I took Mary to Ireland."And what are you going to do on your 50th?" asked the Msgr. "Well," said Paddy "I think I'll bring her back."

Sean and Liam were walking in the woods when they came across a sign saying, "Tree Fellers wanted". Liam says to Sean, "Now isn't that a shame. If Seamus was with us, we could have gotten the job".

A Texas rancher comes to Ireland and meets a Kerry farmer.The Texan says : "Takes me a whole day to drive from one side of my ranch to the other." The Kerry farmer says: "Ah sure, I know, sir. We have tractors like that here too."

One Irishman was explaining to the other how the Lord often compensates for a person's natural deficiencies. "You see," he said, "If someone is a bit blind he might have a very good sense of hearing, or if his sense of taste has gone, he may have a keen sense of smell." "I agree with you," said the other. "I've always noticed that if someone has one short leg, the other one is always just that little bit longer."

A Kerryman and an American were sitting at the Shannon Airport."I've come to meet me brother", said the Kerryman, "he's due to fly in from America in an hour's time. It's his first trip home in fortyyears." "Will you be able to recognize him?" asked the American. "I'm sure I won't", said the Kerryman, "after all these years."“I wonder if he will recognize you?" said the American. "Of course he will". Said the Kerryman, "sure I haven't been away at all."

The warden catches Seamus leaving the vicinity of the reservoir with a bucket of fish. "Aha! I've caught you poachin' fish red-handed," says the warden. "What do you mean, red-handed?" says Seamus. "You've got a bucket full of 'em right there. You can't talk your way out of it this time." "Oh, you don't understand," says Seamus, "I've not poached a thing. These are me pet fish. I bring 'em to the reservoir once a week for exercise. After they've had a good swim, they come back to the bucket and we go back home." "Do ya expect me to believe such an outlandish tale?" "I can prove it." say Seamus. So they walk back to the reservoir and Seamus dips the bucket in and the fish swim away. They stand in silence for 20, 30, 40 minutes - no sign of the fish coming back to the pail. “Ha, ya lying rogue!” shouts the warden. “Where are your fish?” “What fish?”

St. Brigid dies and goes to Heaven. God greets her at the Pearly Gates.”Be thou hungry, Brigid?” asks God. “I could eat,” says she. So God opens a can of tuna, reaches for a chunk of dry bread and they share it. While eating this humble meal, St. Brigid looks down into Hell and sees the inhabitants devouring huge steaks, lobsters, pheasants, pastries, and wines. Curious, but deeply trusting, she remains quiet. The next day God again invites her to join him for a meal. As before, it is tuna and dry bread. Once again, St. Brigid can see the denizens of Hell enjoying smoked salmon, roast lamb, Guinness and Irish whiskey cake. Still she says nothing. The following day, mealtime arrives and another can of tuna is opened. She cannot contain herself any longer. Meekly, she says: “God, I am grateful to be in Heaven with you as a reward for my life of piety, obedience and generosity. But here in Heaven all I get to eat is tuna and bread and in the Other Place they eat like emperors and kings!

I just don't understand..."God sighs. "Let's be honest," he says, "for just the two of us, does it pay to cook?"

Irish patient to fellow in the next bed, "Look, the doctor's coming round soon. Try to cheer him up because he's very worried about you."

An deireadh

Made in the USA
Las Vegas, NV
28 January 2024

85025167R00066